Feng Shui for Wellness and Wealth

Simple Feng Shui Tricks for Personal and Professional Success: Health, Money and Happiness with Feng Shui Tips for Work and Home

By James Adler

Copyright © 2013, 2016

www.YourWellnessBooks.com

Introduction

Thank you for purchasing the book: *Feng Shui for Wellness and Wealth.*

These days, so many people want to practice Feng Shui in their homes and offices because they believe it will make their lives better. Unfortunately, Feng Shui is also subject to so many misunderstandings since there are many people who don't really know what this age-old practice is really about. To be honest, the first time I heard about Feng Shui, I felt skeptic ("does it really work?), and then when I began learning what it was all about, I felt a bit overwhelmed. I thought that it was too much information to absorb and to apply, so I became a little bit discouraged in the process that was "on" and "off" experience. I was trying to do my best to Feng Shui my home and my life once in a while, and then I was back to unhealthy habits. So all my hard work would be for nothing.

This is why I wrote this book, I don't want you to go through the same process. This is a perfect guide for beginners; if you have never heard of Feng Shui or are new to it, you have just found your book. If, on the other hand, you already know something about it, I hope that it can serve as a refresher and motivate you to stick to your Feng Shui lifestyle.

This book will help you to understand just what Feng Shui is, so that you can use the principles of this traditional Chinese practice to create a more harmonious home and office that will not only promote increased success but also help ensure better relationships between people. You will see that Feng Shui is actually very easy to get started on. Once you have started attracting all the good things into your life, it will be like a success magnet!

It is well-known and accepted in the east that the way a particular environment is set up can affect the way that people within it feel, and even act. In the west, however, this belief is often dismissed as superstition. After all, how can interior decoration have an effect on people? But this belief has become increasingly validated by research. For example, it has become widely accepted that the primary color scheme of a room has an effect on the mood of people inside it.

To illustrate, many police departments now have holding cells and booking areas that are colored pink. This is because many experts believe that pink causes a passive response, making it easier to subdue prisoners. Blues and greens are also believed to be the most relaxing colors, which is why they are used in hospitals and testing centers to ease people's nerves. Surgeons wear green-colored scrubs in order to reassure patients.

My own personal experience was that, ever since I discovered Feng Shui, I have managed to actually use it to improve my life in many ways. For example, since I used the principles of Feng Shui to rearrange the environment of my home and office, I have felt lighter and more positive. This has allowed me to become more productive and earn more money, but at the same time, have more free time for myself and my family. And of course, I have more fun since my living environment has become more positive. Now, I can't imagine myself living and working in unorganized and unclean environments. Feng Shui has become a part of my lifestyle. Whenever I visit a friend in their new house, I always start talking about Feng Shui. Most of my family and friends got used to it as they know that I am a 'Feng Shui' nut. Some people love it, some people hate it. I hope that you can make a positive decision of TRANSFORMATION, and choose to be in the category of Feng Shui lovers.

It takes some time and dedication to start to 'Feng Shui' things up, but it's also lots of fun. As one of my Feng Shui gurus, Marie Diamond says, (paraphrasing):*One needs to show the Universe what they want.*

This is the first lesson for you: think of what you REALLY want. Write it down. Include Health, Wealth, Love, Professional Success, Relationships. Make a list of your wishes. Then, using some of the Feng Shui tricks described in this book, show the Universe what you want. Your house and your office will reflect your wishes. As soon as the Universe notices them, the magic will begin.

Sounds weird? Well, you don't need to believe in Feng Shui to practice it. Simply read on and find out for yourself!

This book is perfect for busy westerners, it's short and sweet and packed with basic information that you need to apply to Feng Shui in your home and your life. I am sure you will have fun with it!

Thanks again for downloading this book, I hope you enjoy it!

Chapter 1: What Is Feng Shui?

There are a lot of misconceptions about Feng Shui that prevent people from completely understanding just what this traditional Chinese practice is and what it can do for them. One of the biggest mistaken beliefs about Feng Shui is that it is a quick way to improve luck in your home or office, a belief that many so-called practitioners actually encourage. This is not to say that the practice cannot help bring in more financial and success opportunities by encouraging positive thinking and a more harmonious environment, but Feng Shui is not a magical practice that will automatically bring this about without you having to do anything. While Feng Shui can make it easier for opportunities to approach you, you will still have to work to attract them.

In addition, there is also a prevalent belief that Feng Shui is something that only rich people can practice, another belief that is promoted by many other 'experts'. In fact, anybody can practice Feng Shui if they understand its basic principles. You don't need to buy any expensive 'cures' or other special equipment to practice Feng Shui in your home. I live in a really small apartment. Yet I am able to practice Feng Shui as much as I want to.

So what exactly is Feng Shui? Put simply, Feng Shui looks at the way people interact with their environments and looks for ways to improve them in consonance with the principles of natural energy flow. By enabling the flow of energy in your surroundings, you can achieve certain life improvements by improving the **flow of your own personal energy**.

The way that Feng Shui makes these improvements is by looking at the way your possessions and furniture are placed within the space, and then moving or placing them in order to achieve balance and harmony. The practice was developed by the Chinese, who have been using it for centuries in order to create environments that enhance the possibility of **success in life**.

The name Feng Shui is a combination of two words: *Feng* (wind) and *Shui* (water). These two elements are seen as being vital to human survival, and thus, are carriers of 'chi' or life force. Thus, the practice of Feng Shui involves designing environments in order to improve the flow of chi.

One of the basic things that you can do to start the process of Feng Shui in your home or office is to remove the clutter from these spaces. When your home or office is filled with possessions that you do not use, need or want, it blocks the natural flow of chi through these spaces. Of course, decluttering these spaces is difficult, particularly if the clutter has been allowed to build up over a long time. But it can be done.

One way to approach 'de-cluttering', so that it won't be overwhelming, is to do it step by step. You can devote thirty minutes a day to removing the clutter, and then stop when the time is up. Continue the next day with another session until the room has been cleared, and then move on to the next one. You can also make the task more pleasant by bringing in a sense of positive energy to the task. Open the windows to allow fresh air to come in, and then play some soothing music while you are working. Work with aromatherapy oils or natural incenses to bring some pleasant and harmonious fragrances. Before you know it, you'll be done with the task without feeling heavy or unpleasant. Once you have removed all the clutter from your environment, you'll be surprised at how much lighter you feel and how you seem to have more energy when you're in that space.

Imagine that your flat/ house/ office is a living organism. Imagine that it is not feeling well at all, you can even imagine that it is disease-stricken. Keep repeating to yourself:

I am a healer. I restore balance where there is imbalance!

As soon as you remove all the clutter (in our visualization technique, clutter can be seen as bacteria), your space will be healed and will attract only good energies that you need so much.

Yes! You will be attracting your personal and professional success with your own hands!

Chapter 2: Your Office

Using Feng Shui principles in your office is very important in order to ensure that your personal *chi* is in harmony with your surroundings, which will help you become more efficient and more productive. Unless you have your own office, there are only a limited number of things that you can do to arrange the furnishings in your work space. Nevertheless, there are some things that you can do to create better Feng Shui.

For your cubicle:

- First of all, organize your work space to ensure that it is neat. For example, don't leave files that you are not using lying around, but instead, return them to the proper cabinet. Avoid having excess clutter on your desk. In particular, remove old items that are no longer useful or things that carry bad memories, such as reports that were rejected.

- As much as possible, move your desk in such a way that you can see the entrance to your cubicle. Place a poster of an earth element, such as a forest or canyon, on the wall behind you. If you cannot move your desk, place a small mirror on it in such a way that you can see if someone is approaching.

 Mirrors play an important part in an intelligent Feng Shui-friendly design.

- Place a plant in a red pot, such as a money tree or a small bamboo, at the east side of your desk to energize your work space. Avoid sharp plants such as cacti since they generate bad chi. In addition, you can place good fortune symbols such as a dragon, turtle, or unicorn, around your cubicle or desk.

15

- Put your computer on the west side of your desk to encourage creativity or on the southeast side to promote increased income.

- Place red objects on your desk at the south corner to ensure that you are recognized for your good work. Alternately, you can place a crystal in the south to achieve the same effect.

For your office:

- Make sure that when a visitor enters your office, they see something pleasant such as a healthy plant, since this creates positive chi. You can also put a small fountain near the entrance since this can help improve your mood as well as help generate more income.

- Don't allow clutter or defective equipment to stay in your office. Have them removed. If they cannot be removed at once, place them somewhere, such as a closet, where they are not visible. For the same reason, you should have electrical cords and cables neatly tucked away, since they create a sense of disorder.

- Place equipment such as computers and telephones in the southeast (or wealth) area to encourage increased business to come in.

- If possible, place an aquarium in the north corner of your office to promote increased business success. Put black and blue fish in it, since they absorb negative *chi*.

- Don't place mirrors in the reception area, since these will reflect *chi* back out of your office.

Other tips for your office:

-If there are no windows in your office, or natural light is very limited, consider: painting your office in vibrant colors (some nice, bright tone of blue would be perfect, blue color is said to contain the "metal" elements that bring clarity of thought and abundance), equipping it with more artificial light if necessary, spicing up the atmosphere with essential oils such as lemon, peppermint, orange, sage, and rosemary.

-Use art that can inspire you and motivate you to work. It could be anything that reminds you of your passion and your purpose behind your work. For example, I have my kids' drawings! They are really vibrant and energizing for me, and also, when I work, I constantly remind myself that I also do it to provide for my family.

-Use crystals; whether you believe it or not, crystals are energy and vibration. I recommend you get at least one of the following crystals and keep it in your office:

Citrine (it is great for balancing your ambitions and improving your self-confidence; just press it against your solar plexus when you feel low in energy or disheartened.)

Tigers Eye (it increases focus, clarity of thought, as well as creativity—all you need to work in a productive way!)

Pyrite (it promotes optimism and creativity; helps get you grounded.)

Hematite (it can help you calm down as well as protect your business and home; it's quite affordable. I have one in my car and the other one in my office, I usually keep it on my desk, or I sometimes place it on a shelf.)

A few interesting facts on Feng Shui and the Law of Attraction:

One of the most important tools in Feng Shui is the compass since you can use it to determine the different directions in your office. Every direction has a different type of energy associated with it, and by placing the proper objects in these positions, you can promote the desired effect.

General Directions:

North: career

South: Reputation

West: Creativity and children

East: Family and health

Northeast: Knowledge

Northwest: Helpful people and travel

Southeast: Wealth

Southwest: Love and relationships

I suggest you take a piece of paper, and write down all the areas of your life that needs improvement, e.g.:

> -I want to travel to exotic countries at least twice a year;
>
> -I want to live a healthy and balanced life;
>
> -I want to attract more romance in my life and attract the opposite sex like a magnet.

Now analyze the current organization of your house or apartment. Before we actually get started on specific Feng Shui steps for different areas of your life and your house, I would like you to use your intuition. Let's say that you are looking for wealth and abundance: how does the southeast part of your apartment or office reflect what you want? Maybe it's full of clutter and just totally disorganized? I strongly suggest you do this exercise just using your intuition and common sense. Write down your thoughts, and then compare them with my instructions from the next chapters of this book. Also, ask yourself how you could improve the given part of your house or office simply following your intuition. A really fun task to do, so make sure you don't skip it!

From my own experience:

When I originally got started on Feng Shui, I wanted to attract more romance into my life. I therefore revised the southwest part of my apartment, especially my bedroom. I had been making a horrible mistake of accumulating all the 'old bachelor's stuff' as well as 'little boy's stuff', like for example: some awards from Junior High and pictures from my favorite football matches that I watched with my buddies. No wonder all the females were avoiding me. I was making it obvious to the Universe: I want to carry on the way I live and just hang out with my male friends and watch football!

It wasn't until I removed all the clutter that had been accumulating there for years and made the whole area clean that I could finally create some positive energy around. I simply used my imagination as this is what my Feng Shui coach suggested. He asked me: *If you had a girlfriend or a lover, how would you re-organize your flat/ bedroom to create an atmosphere for lovers rather than for school boys or old bachelors?*

What I did was simple: I set up a mini table with a CD player, and I purchased lots of relaxation and massage music CDs. I also got cinnamon incense sticks and got the hottest aromatherapy oils for lovers that exist: ylang-ylang and cedar wood. I just knew that this new 'decor' would show the Universe what I wanted. I also felt that I was getting enough confidence. Then, I would gradually transform myself from a lonely and depressed man to a man that could actually get to enjoy female company and touch whenever he wanted.

I know that it all seems very simple and logical, but trust me—very few people practice it. Transform your living and working space, and let it transform yourself the way you have always wanted! It won't be an overnight success; just as I said before, it requires some time and dedication. But if it worked for me, it can also work for you. The list of unfulfilled wishes can be a really long one, luckily, there is something that can be done to make them all FULFILLED!

Chapter 3: Your Bedroom

Your bedroom should be your sanctuary, your refuge from the world. However, instead of being that way, our bedroom often becomes an extension of our living room and office, a place where we finish work we take home on our laptops as well as enjoying other leisure activities such as watching TV and playing video games. We should stop this practice, and instead, use the bedroom for what it was intended for, a place for us to rest and sleep, relax as well, as to make passionate love.

Thus, the first Feng Shui tip for the bedroom is, not surprisingly, to remove everything that is not related to sleeping. Put your TV and your game console in your living room, keep your laptop or netbook in its bag, and simply have a bed in your bedroom as well as related furnishings, such as a bedside table and lamp. Keep your bedroom free of clutter. This also goes for the space underneath the bed, which is often used as an impromptu storage space. Put only items that you need and will regularly use, such as shoes, under the bed.

The correct position of your bed is also important. According to the principles of Feng Shui, the bed should not be positioned directly in front of the door, although the door should be visible from your bed. One good position is the corner of the bedroom opposite the door. In addition, the foot of the bed should not point to the bedroom door since it is not conducive to a restful sleep. If your bedroom is small and there is no other way to position your bed, you can ameliorate the effects of the bad position by putting a high footboard or table at the foot of the bed; but it should not be too high that you can no longer see the door.

If there are windows in your bedroom, another no-no is to put the bed in front of the window, particularly if your head is facing it, since it can cause chi to escape. When you wake up, you may find that you feel tired instead of rested.

The position of mirrors in the bedroom can also affect its chi. You should avoid putting a mirror directly opposite the bed in such a way that the sleeper can see him or herself in it. This is believed to cause the chi to bounce around the bedroom, resulting in the sleeper worrying excessively in addition to having trouble sleeping. Another bad position for a mirror is on the wall directly above or opposite your bed, since this is believed to encourage the entrance of a third party into the marriage.

In addition, there should be no images of water in the bedroom. While these are generally considered fortunate for money luck, in the bedroom, water images are seen to possibly promote relationship or financial losses. Instead, choose a piece of art that soothes you, and put it in front of the bed or just opposite it in such a position that it will be the first thing you see in the morning. If feasible, paint your bedroom in a mix of soothing pastel colors and earth tones that promote restfulness and relaxation. The colors that Feng Shui experts recommend, are a range of colors that resemble different tones of human skin, from white to chocolate brown. It is said to stimulate healing and relaxation. Avoid colors that represent the element of metal in Feng Shui, such colors are for example blue, navy blue, and black. These are great for your office, but you need to create a different kind of energy in your bedroom, something that helps you disconnect and relax in a holistic way. If you really like blue, or you already have some blue colors in your bedroom and don't feel like changing it, there is a simple solution. You can balance it by bringing colors from the opposite elements, that is—fire. Do you remember my story of an old and lonely bachelor? My bedroom used to be all blue, from the walls to the pillows. I decided to experiment and balance it with some red (not too much of course). I only added a few redish elements, for example, pillows. I really felt like I spiced it up and added some well-deserved balance. I also got another set of pillows, so as to arrange my bed for two. If you show the Universe what you want, it will come. Feng Shui is one of the ways to manifest your dreams, goals, and desires.

If a couple is sharing the bedroom, the accessories they have should be paired, i.e. identical bedside tables, to reflect their togetherness. In addition, you should avoid furniture with sharp edges such as square tables and choose instead to have rounded or oval ones. Sharp edges can cause cutting chi to focus towards the sleeping couple.

Feng Shuing your bedroom first is, in my opinion, extremely important. The reason is very simple: you need to feel healthy, balanced, and energetic first, so that you can start working on improving other areas of your life. Create your relaxation and sleep clutter-free and chi-promoting environment, and the rest will fall into place!

Additional tips for your bedroom:

-Remember to ventilate it regularly so as to let some fresh oxygen in. Oxygen means the healing energy and vitality!

-Many people think that putting exaggerated amounts of flowers is great for Feng Shui in their bedroom, but the truth is that this is a common misconception. I was very surprised when one of my Feng Shui teachers told me that, in general, plants are not a good element in your bedroom, and that the only exception is if your bedroom is large, and you place them as far from your bed as you possibly can. An interesting fact, isn't it?

-Aromatherapy tips for your bedroom- you may get a few soothing essential oils that promote sleep and relaxation and out a few drops on your pillow or use a diffuser. You can also mix a few drops of your favorite essential oil, and mix it with about 2 tablespoons of a carrier base oil (for example, coconut oil or sweet almond oil). The essential oils that I recommend are: lavanda, lavandin, verbena, palmarosa, as well as ylang-ylang (this one is an aphrodisiac) and cinnamon (this one is an aphrodisiac as well).

-Again, no clutter. I used to leave my clothes all over the place. It took me a while to get myself into the new habit of making the bed, and also picking up all y clothes and placing them in a wardrobe. Now, my bedroom looks perfect. I don't feel stressed out just looking at the mess that I produced. It is also a great time saver.

-Your bed is also important, it is very often overlooked, but Feng Shui recommends a bed with really solid headboard and supportive mattress. You deserve to sleep like a king! I have seen people using mattresses only, without even bothering to use any bed-resembling construction. This is a big mistake, sleeping on a mattress alone is not enough? You should get a proper bed, and it is also important that there is no clutter accumulating underneath it. Also, remove the dust and clean the floor on the regular basis. Make your bedroom healthy, and it will make you healthy and balanced too! Big changes can come from there!

-If you want to attract romance and passion, add some elements (like for example curtains or cushions) in the following colors: red, orange, and pink.

-Use soft lights; candles are the best. You can also use soft, aromatherapy candles.

-Avoid too many portraits or family pictures. They can make you feel overwhelmed as if someone is watching you 24/7!

-As for art, I recommend you include some calming pictures of nature, you can also use some kind of art that inspires you to get up in the morning; use your imagination!

-A few more words on colors that represent the element of metal, even though these are not usually recommended, if you are looking for some clarity of thought or have problems with concentration and focus, you may consider adding some elements in metal element colors such as white, grey, or light blue. I suggest you do it if you already feel fulfilled with love and passion, but maybe you are looking for more ability to focus and think clearly. It is also recommended if you think that your love life is too intense and you wish to calm it down a bit. I think that colors make sense, do you agree with me...?

-Consider getting a few crystals that stimulate healing and relaxation for example:

1.Rose quartz- it is said to have romance and love attracting properties, and it also helps couples stimulate passion and mutual attraction.

2.Howlite- it is a really powerful crystal that you can keep on your night table. If your mind wanders too much, and you have trouble kicking the sack, its vibrations can help you find peace and holistic harmony.

3. Amethyst- it stimulates sleep, I recommend it for those who usually wake up in the middle of the night and can't fall asleep again.

4. Blue Calcite- it promotes body and mind relaxation, healing, and disconnecting from one's thoughts. I use it for meditation.

If you really want to feel at peace in your bedroom, you may also experiment and create your little crystal healing corner or altar; yes I know it does sound weird. The point is to show the Universe how much you want to attract healing and tranquility. Ever since I created my mini meditation corner in my bedroom, I feel amazingly relaxed the moment I enter in. Maybe it's the placebo effect—who knows—but I feel like a warm wave of peace is entering my body when I am in my Feng Shui friendly bedroom. I strongly encourage you to experiment and create peace for yourself and your family.

Chapter 4: Your Kitchen

Your kitchen is one of the most important rooms in your house, since it is the place where you prepare nourishing food for yourself and your family, so you should use Feng Shui principles to bring harmony to it and ensure the free flow of healing *chi*. In my opinion, your kitchen should be arranged in a way that also encourages you to cook and eat in a healthy way. I think that a messy and dirty kitchen naturally tells you to stick to unhealthy food choices, and we don't want that, do we?

As with every other room, the first step is always to organize your kitchen. This not only helps chi flow more freely, it also makes cooking easier since you know where everything is and would have no problem finding it when you're getting ready to cook. Clear your cabinets of old items that you no longer use, as well as spoiled ingredients. Then, put aside things that are still useful but you don't use on a regular basis, so they won't clutter up your countertop. Avoid leaving knives lying around, but put them back in knife blocks after using them.

Once your counters are cleared, add a touch of positive energy to your kitchen by putting in a vase with fresh flowers. Make sure that you change the flowers regularly and remove dead flowers immediately. Alternately, you can put a bowl of fresh fruit on the counter. This will also provide a great incentive for members of the family to pick up a healthy piece of fruit as a snack rather than reaching for junk foods.

In addition, try to keep your kitchen as airy and spacious as possible. If the kitchen has windows, throw them open to let light and positive chi in. A light and spacious kitchen is not only more pleasant to work in; it is also safer, since you can move around more easily without obstruction. If you hang pots and pans on overhead hooks, you should consider removing them to add to the light feel of the room.

The stoves and burners that the cook is using should also be positioned in what is called the 'empowered' position, facing the door of the kitchen. If this is not possible, the cook can place a mirror behind the stove, so he or she can see what is going on behind them (the same mirror trick that we have used for your office).

If you are remodeling your kitchen, repaint it in airy colors such as yellow, since these are good for aiding digestion. In addition, you should add a touch of the earth element to the kitchen by redoing your counter tops in earth colors. For example, you can use brown tiles or concrete for your counters.

If you are living in an apartment that has a small kitchen, and your options for redesigning it are limited, there are still several things that you can do to add positive Feng Shui to the room. For example, use open cabinets with no doors, since this helps to make the chi flow more freely. In addition, you can paint your kitchen in a lighter color.

You can also help expand the kitchen by using mirrors that reflect light and give the illusion of increased space in the area; and in a smaller kitchen, light is important, so avoid just using bland overhead lighting that can drain your energy. Instead, experiment with having several light sources as well as different levels of lighting to see which one brings more energy to your kitchen.

As soon as you re-organize your kitchen and turn it into a clean and healthy 'lab', you will feel more motivated to prepare highly nutritious meals for yourself, your friends, and your family.

From my own experience, I know that it can be really hard to keep the kitchen clean. Especially if you love cooking, like me. When dealing with procrastination, remember to use the 'healing' strategy that I suggested in chapter one. Imagine that your kitchen is a living organism that needs to be 'fixed'. Remove all the 'bacteria', and let it be healthy the way it deserves. If you start applying this strategy, cleaning will become a regular habit of yours. It will become automatic for you. There's no a better feeling than getting up in the morning and starting a day in a clean and health-attracting kitchen!

More Feng Shui tips for your kitchen:

-Your kitchen should create an atmosphere of warmth, not coldness. I know many people who spent lots of money on the latest tech-like 21 st century designs, which may look nice and neat but also extremely cold. One of the basic Feng Shui rules tells you to create warmth in your kitchen. If your kitchen, or kitchen design is too cold, spice it up with some warm-colored elements, towels, curtains, or flowers (e.g. yellow, orange, and warm green). You may also experiment with the lights.

- The food that you store in your kitchen also influences its energy. I suggest you reduce or at least try to eliminate processed foods and fast food. I am not telling you to go vegetarian, but in my own personal opinion, the less meat you store in your kitchen (and eat) the better.

-A nicely balanced, Feng Shui kitchen is also associated with herbal scents and natural fragrances. I love to use natural essential oils like basil, rosemary, clove, and mint. Sometimes, I even use a few drops of each. I like to use natural tea tree oil for cleaning. It helps kill bacteria, is natural, and leaves an amazingly fresh and energizing, warm scent. Other oils that I recommend for your kitchen atmosphere are fennel, cypress, and juniper. They all have a nice foresty-herbal like scent.

-I am sure that after reading the previous chapters, you are also wondering whether James will come up with any healing crystals for your kitchen. Here are some of my favorites:

1. Carnelian

2. Garnet

3. Red Jasper

4. Ruby

The reason why they will work for balancing your kitchen is that they have nice and warm colors to spice things up, stimulate the digestive power, and also can increase your cooking creativity and health motivation.

-An interesting fact that I never really paid attention to, even though I have always enjoyed cooking, you can also create Feng Shui on your plates! If possible, try to use plates in warm colors (orange, yellow, green, and warm brown), and pay attention to the way you arrange foods on your plate. For example, I used to be really lazy about it, it wasn't until one of my Macrobiotic Diet teachers pointed out to it as a fundamental error. It took me a while to understand that all details count. It's not only about what you eat, it's also about how you prepare it and how you serve it. Live and eat like a king (or a queen!).

-Not only does a nice and balanced kitchen attract more wellness and health, but it also attracts wealth and productivity. We are talking about the place where you fuel your body and mind, so that they work on their optimal levels and feel great. When you feel great, you have more energy, and not only can you attract good things, but you also take action and come up with the best plan ever to make your dreams come true. There is the old Chinese proverb that says: "Your health is your wealth"! I actually have a picture with that proverb written in Chinese. It's on my kitchen table, and it serves me as a constant reminder to take care of myself to be able to achieve my financial goals as well.

-There is a Feng Shui challenge that I really encourage you to do, as much as you can. I know that it can be difficult at first, but it basically tells you to turn off the TV when you're eating. Yes! It promotes mindful eating. It was a really big challenge for me, but now I am used to eating with some gentle music in the background and also candles (another symbol of the fire element that is great for digestion and attracting abundance). Mindful eating helps you feel more grounded, and so it works in accordance with the earth element that is crucial for the Feng Shui in your kitchen.

If you have problems with mindfulness while eating, try to use earth elements the other way round; add some elements with earth-like colors, for example brown. These can be plates, spoons, forks, cups, and serviettes...Music that is nice, warming, and relaxing can also help you to achieve mindful eating. Feng Shui works with all senses!

Chapter 5: Your Living Room

The living room is the place where your family spends most of their time when they are at home, so the chi should flow freely around it. Again, you should begin by ensuring that the room is spacious, so that the chi can move around freely. Apart from not having too much furniture in it, you should remove clutter, such as old newspapers and other junk that is no longer being used.

When you are deciding how to place or move the furniture in your living room to ensure the free movement of chi, try this exercise. Stand in the middle of the room and look at the entrance. Imagine the chi as water flowing from the door. Does it flow freely from the door to the various places in the room? Or are there things that are blocking it? If so, these are the things that you should move.

Since you want to encourage people to hang out in the living room, you should put comfortable chairs and sofas in it. Avoid furniture that has sharp corners and edges. You can also put healthy plants on the corners of the room to soften them. If there are windows, you should pull back the drapes to let in light and as much as possible; open them to make the room airy.

Add to the positive feeling in the room by putting fresh flowers in a vase on a table. Another thing that you can do to facilitate the movement of chi in the room is to keep a small fountain with running water. Then, add the element of wood by using wooden furniture such as wood side tables and chairs. If there are cabinets or bookshelves in the room, make sure they have glass doors or are open.

The sofa, which is the main piece of furniture in the room, should be placed correctly. It should have a clear view of the door and should not be facing it. In addition, the sofa should be placed in the corner of the room that is farthest from the door and window. Don't put the sofa too close to the wall, since the wall symbolizes a sense of security and protection. To reinforce the sense of security, choose furniture that has high backs. Place other furniture along the walls of the room, and keep the center clear in order to facilitate the movement of chi.

When deciding on the colors of the room, use a neutral color scheme such as white or yellow, and add touches of brighter colors using the curtains, rugs, and pictures. For example, to add the element of fire in the room, use curtains in red or strong yellow. You can also add earth colors such as brown and mustard, but don't overdo it, since this can sap people's energy.

As much as possible, you should also have several levels of lighting in the room, apart from the central overhead lighting. When family or friends are hanging out in the room, you can use strong lighting. If couples and smaller groups are in the room, you should use softer lighting. If the room has dark corners, you can correct this by using lamps to brighten them.

When decorating the room, make sure it is filled with things that evoke positive feelings or associations, such as pictures of the family or keepsakes that are associated with pleasant memories.

More Feng Shui tips for your living room:

-Employ aromatherapy that has energizing and uplifting properties. I love it when I have family and friends visiting my place, and the moment they step in my living room they say: "Wow, it smells so nice!" I generally use citrus oils such as lemon, orange, mandarin, palmarosa, and bergamot. Everyone loves them! You may also try fragrances such as geranium, patchouli, rose or lemongrass. Use them in vaporizers or diffusers.

-Create a nice and cozy atmosphere that also helps possible guests feel like at home and socialize. All details count, even the fabrics. Try to cover the sofa with something that is nice to touch and sit on. Something that is friendly for the skin and for the senses.

-When you see on the sofa, you should be able to see and control the entry as well as not have any items or furniture behind you. If you can't move your sofa, try using a mirror, so that you can control and see everything, just like a king!

-TV as well as other electronic devices are bad for Feng Shui, but there are a few trick that you can use to balance it. For example, get a few, natural aromatherapy candles and a few books. These will create a non-technology environment and boost relaxation as well as communication. It will also help you realize that the living room is not only about watching TV, and will hopefully help you communicate better with your family and friends.

-If you don't have a fireplace, get some candles or some kind of art that resembles a fireplace, which represents a happy and balanced home and the sense of coziness.

-As far as crystals are concerned, you want those who attract protection, health, and communication. The crystals that I recommend are:

1. Amethyst- it gives you strength to be positive, even if you are exposed to negativity.

2. Black Tourmaline- I recommend you expose it to a visible place in your living room, if there is are negative persons entering your home.

3. Smokey Quartz- it helps fight fear and anxiety as well as obsessive worrying.

4. Selenite- it stimulates protection as well as the sensation of peace. It clears negative environment vibrations and negative thoughts that you may get exposed to. It's a great crystal to have for your kids' room as well.

- Our Paleolithic ancestors would gather with their tribes around the fire which was like a focus point. This is exactly the way it should be in the 21st century. We have much more comfortable equipment now, but very often, we forget about the basics. Aim to create your own focus point, where family members and friends sit down and relax, feeling warm and protected. As far as TV is concerned—don't let it be the focus point. Use it occasionally as an addition. Choose movies that the whole family can enjoy.

Chapter 6: Your Bathroom

In Feng Shui, the bathroom is considered one of the dirtiest rooms in the house due to the flow of water out of the house. Remember that the goal of Feng Shui is to encourage chi to circulate around the house. However, there are fixes that you can implement that can help neutralize the bad Feng Shui in the bathroom.

In the bathroom, the most problematic item is the toilet, since it is the biggest drain in the room where the most water leaves the bathroom. In addition, the flush creates a powerful suction that pulls down the energy with it. One of the simplest ways that you can prevent chi from leaving is to simply keep the toilet lid closed, particularly when you are flushing the toilet. For the same reason you should keep the shower curtains closed since the shower also has a drain. If you can, you should also pop the drains closed after you finish using the tub or shower using plastic drain covers, which prevents the chi from escaping.

If you are still designing your bathroom, you can either segregate the toilet by giving it its own space with a separate door, or if the toilet has to be in the same room as the sink and shower, try to position it in such a way that it is as far from the bathroom door as possible.

You can also put a large mirror in the bathroom in order to help the energy to circulate and speed up; but you should ensure that the mirror does not reflect the toilet, since this would have the opposite effect. When you are sitting on the toilet, you should not be able to see your entire body in the mirror.

In addition, unless your bathroom looks unsightly, you can keep the door open to let the chi circulate. However, there are some times when the door should be closed as much as possible. If the door of the bathroom is in a direct line with the main door of the house, it should be closed to prevent the chi entering your home from flushing down the toilet. In fact, if you can, you should install a tension rod to ensure the door automatically closes. If the toilet is near the kitchen, you should also keep the door closed at all times. Finally, if you can see the toilet from your bed, you should keep it closed at night before going to bed, so that it won't be the first thing you see when you wake up in the morning.

Since the bathroom has an excess of the water element, you should balance it out by adding the earth element. You can do this by painting the walls in earth colors such as yellow and gold. Alternately, you can use towels, accessories and pictures with these colors. For smaller bathrooms, you can paint them in darker earth colors such as brown and brick red, then balance it out with lighter colors such as white.

You can add positive energy to the bathroom by putting in an orchid in a pot. Orchids are the ideal flower to put in the bathroom, since they thrive in moist environments. However, they will still need natural light, so they might be a better choice for bathrooms that have windows. In addition, you can put in attractive accessories to the bathroom that will make you happy when you look at them.

More Feng Shui tips for your bathroom:

-Bathroom is like SPA to me. It's a place for relaxation and rejuvenation. The mere sound of water running down the shower or bath is relaxing to me. To stimulate this feeling, I have a few pictures of nature (waterfalls, lakes, beach, everything that is SPA to me). I encourage you to do the same.

-I use natural and organic cosmetics, mostly aromatherapy and essential oils. My wife and I are pretty hooked on them. Choose essential oils that suit your preferences, and create your own spa. If that sounds interesting, check out my book: "Ayurveda Rocks-Discover Wellness and Healing with Ayurvedic Aromatherapy").

-Use gentle and soothing music in the background, just like at the most luxurious spa. I usually have quite a few playlists on my mobile and choose the one that works for me and for the given moment.

-Use healing colors like blue and green; these can be soap containers or towels, sponges, and other accessories.

-Do not use any images that represent your family, career, relationships, or money. Your bathroom should be like a place where you let things go, a place where you vent negative emotions, and clean your body not only on a physical level, but also emotional and mental.

-Images of trees are an excellent symbol of renewal and strength, so use them in your bathroom to your heart's content.

-Use crystals that stimulate healing and relaxation. I especially recommend:

1. Abalone- great for those, who, just like me, are easily agitated and irritated (yes, I very often just hit the roof!)

2. Larimar- an amazing crystal for those who tend to be moody and change from super excited and happy to bitter and sad for no reason and within less than 5 minutes. Larimar balances, helps ground oneself, heals, and protects. It is great for those who wish to balance and control their emotions.

3. Aventurine- do you like meditation? I do! And I love meditating in my bath too. Aventurine brings about the

wonderful sensation of calm and being connected with the "here and now".

4. Amethyst- I recommend this crystal for those who tend to suffer from tension headaches, and you can also use it for self-massage (just intuitively touch your neck, your occipital bone, your forehead, and your temples).

5. In my bathroom, I have a mini "altar" of the above-mentioned crystals. The feeling that I get is the same when I enter my bedroom. These are my spas and my places for relaxation and rejuvenation. I feel at peace, like everything has meaning, reason, and everything flows in good direction.

A few years ago, my place was full of clutter and extremely disorganized. Ever since I have changed it, I stimulated the process of my personal and professional transformation. I am not saying that Feng Shui is the ultimate cure. But what you feel and experience (here I refer to where you live , that is spend many hours a day and night at), is extremely important to your overall performance, both mental, physical and emotional as well as all your achievements.

Reading this book is only the tip of the iceberg. I hope that it infected some Feng Shui curiosity in you. You now have the basics to get started on Feng Shuing your home and also your life. Big changes can happen from there.

Now, it's time for you to make a move and take action. Once you have done the basics rearrangement in your home, you may go from there and explore more advance resources and take care of some details.

Be aware of everything that happens in your life as well. It's all interconnected. Have a diary or a journal. Think which areas of your life need improve and how you can stimulate it with the ancient art or Feng Shui.

Enjoy!

Conclusion

Thanks again for taking interest in my book. I hope that you found it helpful, and that the overview of Feng Shui that I presented will inspire you take action to *Feng Shui up* your living and working environment.

Now that you've learned some of the techniques that you can use to improve the Feng Shui in your home, why not start using them? You can gradually implement some of them and see how they make your home's chi and your personal chi better. You can even help your friends and family with their homes and offices.

One of the most important things to realize about Feng Shui is that although it started in China, you do not have to use specific Chinese symbols when practicing Feng Shui in your home. What is important is that you understand the basic philosophy behind it and use symbolism that is relevant to your particular culture, which has a particular meaning for you. As long as the environment that you create makes you feel positive, that is what is important.

In line with this, you should use techniques that make you feel good. Don't hesitate to experiment with various methods as well as mixing them up to create a positive living and working environment in which you can thrive and live life to the fullest, as well as do your best work.

Furthermore, if you enjoyed this book, please take the time to share it on social media. It would be greatly appreciated!

Your honest review is a great way to let others know of the benefits you've got from this book. This will not only help others reach their lifestyle goals, but it is incredibly rewarding for me to know how much work has benefited others! This way you can help empower others in the way Feng Shui has empowered you.

Enjoy the journey!

James Adler